SIN WAY

MEDITATIONS
ON THE
WORDS
OF
SAINT FRANCIS

MURRAY BODO, O.F.M.

ST. ANTHONY MESSENGER PRESS
Cincinnati, Ohio

Cover design by Mark Sullivan
Book design by Jennifer Tibbits
Cover image "Francesco" by Mark Balma

LIBRARY OF CONGRESS CATALOGING-IN-PUBLICATION DATA

Bodo, Murray.
  The simple way : meditations on the words of Saint Francis of Assisi / Murray Bodo.
      p. cm.
  Includes bibliographical references and index.
  ISBN 978-0-86716-914-0 (pbk. : alk. paper) 1. Francis, of Assisi, Saint, 1182-1226—Meditations. I. Title.
  BX4700.F6B5558 2009
  242—dc22

                                        2008052276

ISBN 978-0-86716-914-0

Published by St. Anthony Messenger Press
28 W. Liberty St.
Cincinnati, OH 45202
www.SAMPBooks.org

Printed in the United States of America.

Printed on acid-free paper.

09 10 11 12 13 5 4 3 2 1

*To Secular Franciscans and all those who seek
to follow in the footsteps of Saint Francis*

CONTENTS

INTRODUCTION

The Simple Way is meant as a help to meditation, as a book to pray with, and as a personal notebook. Space is provided beneath each meditation to jot down your own thoughts, if you wish, or to insert a prayer of your own. It is small in size so that you can carry it easily in your pocket or purse.

The introductory words and stories of Saint Francis in each reflection are the author's translations from Francis' own Latin or Italian writings.

HOW TO PRAY WITH THIS BOOK

1. Place yourself in the presence of God.
2. Read the words of Saint Francis slowly and prayerfully. What words strike you as important to you personally? Why? Read them again, out loud if you can.
3. Read the meditation provided and ask yourself how you would expand on it from your own experience.
4. Enter into a short time of silence with one thought that struck you in the words of Saint Francis or in the meditation.
5. Thank God for God's inspiration for this day.
6. Answer the question(s) provided in the text for the day.
7. Write your resolution following the words: "Today I will...."

A SIMPLE WAY
TO LOVE GOD

A New Kind of Fool

The Lord called me to the simple and humble way and has indeed made this way known through me and through all those who choose to believe me and follow me. God told me I am to be a new kind of fool in this world.

Saint Francis was the son of one of the richest merchants in Assisi, but he chose gospel poverty over wealth. In so doing he was mocked by many as a fool and madman. And yet others saw that his kind of foolishness was really wisdom.

Saint Francis, they saw, brought love to places there was little or no love, and he found love there. He began to live among the lepers, and a family of love began to emerge. Love begins where we decide to bring love.

Where is there little love in my life and how can I make a difference?

Today I will _____

_____

THOSE WHO ARE DESTINED
FOR ETERNAL LIFE

I ask the sick that in everything you give thanks to the
Creator. And whatever it might be that God wants for
you, whether it is health or sickness, let that be what
you want also; for all those whom God has destined for
eternal life God touches by allowing the allurement of
trials and sickness and compunction of spirit.

The French Catholic novelist Leon Bloy (1846–1917) once
wrote, "There are places in the heart that do not yet exist; suffering has to enter in for them to be."

One of those places in the heart is ongoing gratitude to God for
our very existence. We take this greatest of gifts for granted, and
then God allows what Saint Francis calls the "allurement of trials
and sickness" to enter our lives; and we then either reject God or are
bitter toward God; or we learn gratitude, which expands our hearts
and brings us joy even in the midst of suffering. This does not mean
we take joy in the suffering, but that we take joy in accepting God's
will whose purpose is to lead us to the good God.

How has God used suffering and trials to lead me closer to him?
How have I responded?

Today I will _____

_____

TO KNOW CHRIST

It is good to read the testimony of the Scriptures, and it is good to seek out the Lord our God in them. But as for me, I have already made so much of Sacred Scripture my own that I have more than enough for my meditation and reflection. I have need of nothing more. I know Christ, the poor crucified one.

Saint Francis lived so long with the sacred Scriptures that they became a part of who he was. He so internalized God's Word that it became for him the Word Incarnate, Jesus Christ. Jesus became sufficient Scripture for Saint Francis because Jesus summed up and incarnated all of God's holy Words. But Saint Francis' love for Christ was only possible because he lived out in his own life what the Word of God asked of him. Only one who lives God's Words can really know God's Word, the poor crucified Christ.

How much of what I read or hear of the gospel do I put into practice?

Today I will _____

_____

WEEPING OVER THE PASSION OF CHRIST

> When he was asked why he went about the country-
> side weeping, Saint Francis said, "Because I need to
> travel through the whole world and, without any false
> shame, cry and moan over the passion of my Lord."

Saint Francis' love for Jesus was personal and life-changing. In one of his mystical experiences he was praying before the crucifix of the run-down wayside chapel of San Damiano below Assisi when the image of Christ on the cross spoke to him saying, "Francis, go and repair my house which, as you see, is falling into ruin." And Francis saw that it was true. The house of God was falling into ruin, as was the love for the crucified Savior who had spoken to him.

For the rest of his life, Saint Francis was in love with this poor crucified Savior, not only as he is portrayed in countless crucifixes, but also as he is revealed in the poor person, the outcast, the leper and all those who have been marginalized and rejected as Jesus was. Francis wept for the Passion and death of this Christ, as well as all those who mirror Christ in their suffering.

Do I see the suffering of those around me, and do I see Christ in them?

Today I will _____

_____

A Prayer of Total Love

May the fiery and honey-sweet power of your love, O
Lord, wean me from all things under heaven, so that I
may die for love of your love who deigned to die for
love of my love.

With Saint Francis it's all about love: love returning love.
When he was praying on Mt. La Verna, shortly before he
received the sacred stigmata, Saint Francis prayed for two graces:
that he might experience in his own body the pain and suffering
Christ bore in his Passion, and that he might feel in his heart the
love which moved Jesus to love us even to the point of suffering and
dying for us.

Francis learned in prayer that it was for love of our love that
Jesus suffered what he did. Francis then prayed that he might die
for love of Jesus' love, as Jesus died for love of Francis' love.

What a tremendous lover Saint Francis was to make such a
request and to follow through as he did.

What is my deepest prayer?

Today I will _____

_____

GIVING BIRTH TO CHRIST

O to have a Father in heaven, how glorious and holy and great that is! O to have such a Spouse in heaven, how holy, beautiful, and lovable! O to have such a Brother, how holy and how beloved, how pleasing and lowly, peaceful and sweet and lovable and desirable above all things! And O to have such a Son, who laid down his life for his sheep and who prayed to the Father for us.

What wonderfully intimate and generative language! When Jesus' disciples told him that his mother and brothers were outside waiting for him, Jesus said that his mother and brothers are those who do the will of his Father in heaven.

This image captures Saint Francis' imagination, and he praises God as his spouse, whose embrace makes the virginal heart pregnant with Christ who, in being born again through us, continues to lay down his life and to pray for us.

What do I need to do to give birth to Christ in my life?

Today I will _____

_____

A Reward for Faithfulness

Temptation overcome is the ring by which the Lord espouses the soul.

Again, Saint Francis uses intimate spousal language in speaking of his Lord. Those who overcome temptation are wed to God, and temptation overcome is the ring they wear to prove their betrothal to God. As with many mystics, Saint Francis experiences God so intimately that his relationship with God is likened to married love in which two people become one in their love for one another. Often mystics invoke the Bible's Song of Songs to express their intimacy with God.

What is my image of my relationship with God? What does it move me to do?

Today I will _____

_____

THE DIFFERENCE BETWEEN KNOWING AND DOING

What a great shame that while the saints actually followed in the footsteps of the Lord, we, today's servants of God, expect glory and honor simply because we can recite what they did.

It is much easier to read Bible stories or saints' lives and admire the heroic lives there than to try to be heroic ourselves. Do we think we're not worthy, not brave or good enough? Are we afraid to be as big as we really are? Whatever the reason, we hide our light under a bushel basket, we refuse to believe we are the salt of the earth. Much good is left undone, much intimacy with God is unexplored.

We know what we need to do to help transform our world. We know it is doing God's will that will transform us and our world. Do we choose our own will instead?

Do I try always to put God's will first?

Today I will _____

_____

ADORATION OF THE HOLY EUCHARIST

> Kissing your feet and with all the love I'm capable of,
> I beg you to render, as far as you can, all reverence and
> total adoration to the Most Holy Body and Blood of our
> Lord Jesus Christ, in whom all things in heaven and on
> earth are made peaceful and are reconciled to God the
> Almighty.

Saint Francis singles out again and again in his writings the centrality of the Holy Eucharist, for it is there that the Risen Christ is most tangibly present to us. There is a story that illustrates this dramatically.

Once when he was visiting a town, the citizens brought Saint Francis before their parish priest because, they said, he was living in sin, and they wanted the saint to reprimand him and condemn his sinful way of life.

Instead, Saint Francis fell to his knees before the priest, and taking his hands, said, "I know not whether this priest is sinful. I only know that these hands, and these hands alone, make present upon the altar my Lord and Savior Jesus Christ."

Saint Francis' reverence for the priesthood was first and foremost because of the priest's power to transform bread and wine into the living Resurrected Christ, "in whom all things in heaven and on earth are made peaceful and are reconciled to God the Almighty."

Having heard the words of Saint Francis, and considering my own devotion to Christ in the Eucharist, what am I called to do?

Today I will _____

_____

GOD OF ALL THINGS

All-powerful, most holy, most high and supreme God,
Holy and just Father,
Lord, King of heaven and earth,
we thank you for yourself
for through your holy will
and through your only Son
with the Holy Spirit,
You have created all things spiritual and corporal
and, having made us in your own image and likeness,
You placed us in paradise.
Then, through our own fault, we fell.

At the time of Saint Francis there was a widespread heresy called Catharism, which claimed that the good God created only spirit and that matter was created by the evil god, who through matter causes us to sin. In this prayer Saint Francis corrects this aberration and once again asserts that God is one and has created all things spiritual and material and placed us in a spiritual and material paradise. Nor did the evil god cause us to fall from this original grace—it was through our own fault that we fell.

What is my own attitude to matter, to my own body, particularly? Do I look down upon my body and elevate my soul, or do I believe that everything that God has made is good and that I am made in the image and likeness of God?

Today I will _____

_____

God's Gift of the Incarnation

> We thank you
> that through your Son you created us,
> and through the holy love you had for us
> you brought about his birth
> as true God and true man
> by the glorious, ever-virgin, most blessed, holy Mary,
> and that you willed to redeem us captives
> through his cross and blood and death.

It is a Franciscan teaching that it was not our sin that moved the eternal Christ to come and live among us on earth, that it was not something as negative as sin that motivated God to send his only Son. Christ would have come and lived among us whether or not we had sinned. It was divine love that caused the Incarnation to happen, as Saint Francis says in this writing. But because we had become captive to sin, Christ willed to redeem us through his cross and blood and death.

The Incarnation was in the divine plan from all eternity; that Christ had to suffer and die when he did come, was because of his love for us that was so perfect that he wanted to be like us in all things but sin, thereby redeeming our total humanity and offering it to the

Father as a perfect sacrifice of a human being who was also divine. This is a great mystery that moves Francis to give thanks to God.

When I think about the incredible gift of the Incarnation, what am I moved to do?

Today I will _____

_____

WHAT WE ARE TO GLORY IN

We shouldn't flatter ourselves and boast about doing
what any sinner can do. A sinner can fast, pray, weep,
mortify the flesh. But this a sinner cannot do: Remain
faithful to God. Therefore, this is what we should glory
in: Rendering glory to God, serving God faithfully, and
acknowledging as God's whatever God gives us.

In these words Saint Francis gives us a threefold plan for our life:
(1) *Rendering glory to God.* If in everything praiseworthy that
comes our way, we immediately give the glory to God instead of to
ourselves, we are on the way to true humility. (2) *Serving God faith-fully.* If we place the fulfilling of God's will as the priority of our life,
we are establishing the foundation of all love, both divine and
human. (3) *Acknowledging as God's whatever God gives us.* If we refuse
to be possessive about God's gifts but realize instead that these gifts
have been lent to us by God, the great Almsgiver, then we are well
on the way to the poverty of spirit that Jesus speaks of at the begin-ning of his first sermon which gives us God's kingdom: Blessed are
the poor in spirit, for theirs is the kingdom of heaven.

What do I do with the gifts God has given me and do I remem-ber to remember God who is their source and blessing?

Today I will _____

_____

Mary, God's Womb

How right it is that we honor highly the Virgin Mary, for
she carried Jesus in her most holy womb.

Mary as the womb of God. How greatly honored is she who was chosen by the Father, the Son and the Holy Spirit to be the dwelling place of God become human in Jesus Christ. And how greatly honored are we as human beings, not only because God became one of us, but because God chose one of us to be his womb for nine months of his human life. And, as Saint Francis reminds us in another of his writings, how privileged each one of us is that we, too, can become a womb of God by doing God's will and bringing him to birth in our lives.

How important is Mary to my life and what can I learn from her?

Today I will _____

_____

REVERENCE FOR GOD'S WORDS

I encourage you in Christ to show all possible reverence for
the written words of God wherever you may find them;
and if you come upon God's words, and you see that they
are not being cared for or are piled up haphazardly or are
scattered about, gather them up and care for them; for in
honoring the words, you honor the Lord who spoke them.

When Saint Francis was in Damietta, Egypt during the Fifth
Crusade, he spent over twenty days in the camp of the
Sultan, Malek-al-Kamil, witnessing to Jesus Christ and trying to
bring peace between the crusaders and the Muslims. While there,
Francis was moved by the honor which the Muslims showed to the
ninety-nine names of Allah. It confirmed for him the importance of
reverence for God's name, which he already held dear in his own
heart and life.

Reverence for God's written words. Again and again Saint
Francis admonishes us to hold reverently the words of God which
hold God himself in their mystery. Reverence for the words of God
leads to reverence for *the* Word of God, who is Jesus Christ.

What is my attitude toward the words of God?

Today I will _____

_____

THE IMPORTANCE OF AWARENESS

> If Saint Francis heard people use lightly the words, "For the love of God," he didn't like it and would often rebuke them for it, saying, "The love of God is so exalted that it should be mentioned rarely, in extreme need, with great reverence."

How great must have been Saint Francis' reverence for God's name and God's love! And how brave he was and principled, like the good knight he wanted to become when he was a young man. He speaks out for his liege Lord, who is God himself. He doesn't remain silent when he perceives that his Lord's name and honor is being taken in vain, or spoken of lightly.

How callous we've become. How lightly and sometimes sinfully we utter God's name. And how easily we use God's name and God's attributes to serve our own needs, our own point of view, our own ideology. How many evil things have been done in God's name, and how blissfully we ignore or deny their consequences.

In this writing Saint Francis teaches us how to remedy our carelessness.

How can I become more aware of the importance of reverence for God?

Today I will _____

_____

WHAT GOD DOES FOR US

God gave us and keeps on giving to each one of us a
whole body, a whole soul, a whole life. God created us
and redeemed us and will save us by mercy alone. God
has done and keeps on doing everything good for us.

This passage of Saint Francis echoes the famous passage of Julian
of Norwich, a medieval English mystic who was born a little
over a hundred years after the death of Saint Francis:

> And he showed me... a little thing, the size of a hazelnut, on the
> palm of my hand, round likes a ball. I looked at it thoughtfully
> and wondered, "What is this?" And the answer came, "It is all
> that is made." I marveled that it continued to exist and did not
> suddenly disintegrate; it was so small. And again my mind sup-
> plied the answer: "It exists, both now and for ever, because God
> loves it...." In this "little thing" I saw three truths. The first is
> that God made it; the second is that God loves it; and the third
> is that God sustains it. [1]

We are as small as this thing the size of a hazelnut in comparison to
our Creator. We are a whole body, a whole soul, a whole life only
because of God's mercy and goodness.

What response shall I make to so much goodness and love?

Today I will _____

_____

NOTE

[1] Clifton Wolters, ed. and trans., *Julian of Norwich, Revelations of Divine Love* (New York: Penguin, 1966), pp. 67–68.

THE ONE THING NECESSARY

In holy charity, which God is, I beg all of you that, removing every obstacle and putting aside every worry and every care as best you can, you strive to serve, love, adore, and honor the Lord God with a pure heart and pure mind which is what God asks above all else.

These words of Saint Francis apply as fully today as when he wrote them eight hundred years ago. It is our worry and our cares that so often prevent us from the one thing necessary, the one thing God asks us above all else. Saint Francis and countless good souls since his time have taken the great risk of banking everything on making the first commandment the first principle of everything they are and everything they do. In that commitment their whole life changes into a living example of what it means to love God and neighbor. For to serve, love, adore and honor God with a pure heart and pure mind leads inevitably to love of one's neighbor.

How much time do I spend adoring and loving God?

Today I will _____

_____

Praying the Our Father

Our Father, Holiest One, our Creator, Redeemer, Comforter, who are in heaven, you are in the angels and saints enlightening them to knowledge, for you are light; you inflame them to love, for you are love; you dwell in them and fill them with blessedness, for you are the highest good, the eternal good from whom is all good and without whom there is no good.

These words are from the beginning of Saint Francis' paraphrase of the Our Father. He continues throughout the whole prayer to add his own words to the ones Jesus gave us.

Were I to add my own spontaneous words to the words of the Our Father, what would they be, and what would they lead to in my own way of praying?

Today I will _____

_____

How to Respond to Evil

When we see or hear someone speak or do evil or blaspheme God, let us speak and do what is good and praise God who is blessed forever. Amen.

Counteracting evil with good. It is easy to answer evil with evil; it is hard, and sometimes heroic, to answer evil with good. Saint Francis is a troubadour of the positive, of praise rather than condemnation. In every situation he praises God, even when evil is trying to overcome his attitude of praise and adoration.

How do I react when I see or hear someone speak or do evil?

Today I will _____

_____

A Light in the Darkness

In his courtesy and good pleasure, God can banish
darkness and give us God's own wonder-working light.

Cortesia, courtesy, is the virtue of the knight. Saint Francis attributes the knightly virtue of courtesy to God. Like the good knight, God is kindly disposed toward us, and it is God's good pleasure to fill us with Divine wonder-working light. This is the light that banishes darkness.

God does not violently banish darkness like a ruthless knight, but instead simply fills us with divine light, which darkness cannot abide. This is the light Saint John the Evangelist writes of: "The light shines in the darkness, and the darkness did not overcome it" (John 1:5).

This wonder-working light of God is Jesus Christ. In him there is no darkness.

Do I turn to Christ for light when I am in darkness?

Today I will _____

_____

Seeing the World Right Side Up

Know that there are some things in life that are exalted and sublime before God but are low and despicable in others' eyes; and other things that people consider grand and noble, are counted worthless and vile in the eyes of God.

When Saint Francis renounced his inheritance and gave away all his possessions, then went to live among the lepers, people mocked him and thought him mad, but God saw it all as sublime and admitted Saint Francis to the company of his intimates. On the other hand, when Francis was a young playboy and spendthrift, squandering his father's money on parties and extravagant clothes, God withdrew his intimacy, and Francis was sad and unfulfilled.

Is the way I see the world and my place in it keeping me from intimacy with God?

Today I will _____

_____

MAKING A JOYFUL SOUND

Who are God's servants but God's minstrels who comfort the human heart and lead it to spiritual joy?

When Saint Francis was joyful, he would pick up two sticks from the ground and, playing them like a violin, he would sing in French his praises of God. This gave him so much comfort and spiritual joy that he wanted to share his song with everyone. And if there were no humans there, he would sing to the animals and nature.

What brings me to song? Do I share my joy with others?

Today I will _____

_____

THE DANGER OF SELF-SATISFACTION

My brothers and sisters, let us begin to serve the Lord
God, for up till now we have done little, or nothing.

Like the great apostle Paul, Saint Francis was always pressing on toward the goal—and for the same reason: the love of Christ Jesus. Christ had spoken to Saint Francis to go and repair his church; he had appeared to Francis in a leper. He had spoken to Francis as does a liege lord to his knight telling him not to go to war any longer and giving him a vision of a royal hall with shields that were those of spiritual knights and telling Saint Francis that the shields were for him and his followers if he turned away from war. With so many missions given him by Christ himself, Francis was impelled by love for Christ, who had so gifted him, unworthy though he was.

How has Christ gifted me? And what shall I do to return his love?

Today I will _____

_____

LEARNING TO SEE ARIGHT

> This is how you will know that you have the Spirit of the
> Lord: If when the Lord does something good through you,
> the flesh does not get puffed up (for the flesh is ever in
> opposition to the good); but instead, you remain less in
> your own eyes, less than all other people.

Saint Francis was always aware of the danger of pride, and he
believed the only remedy to be Christ's remedy,

> *who, though he was in the form of God,*
> *did not regard equality with God*
> *as something to be exploited,*
> *but emptied himself,*
> *taking the form of a slave*
> *being born in human likeness,*
> *And being found in human form,*
> *he humbled himself*
> *and became obedient to the point of death—*
> *even death on a cross.* (Philippians 2:6–8)

And so Francis constantly referred all good to God and emptied himself out in the service of others.

How do I counteract pride in my life?

Today I will _____

_____

KEEPING OUR EYES ON JESUS

> The Son of God left the womb of the Father and descended from heaven's height into our misery to teach us by word and example, even he the Lord and Master, what humility is.

Saint Francis kept his eyes ever on Jesus. How did he live? Where did he spend his time? Whom did he single out as his true disciples? What was his relationship with his Father, who had sent him? What did Jesus say we should be? How did he tell us to live? What was the model he gave for his true followers?

In all this Francis saw humility.

What do I see I am to do when I look at Christ, and what do I hear him say that tells me how I should live my life?

Today I will _____

_____

DELIGHTING IN GOD, THREE IN ONE

> Let us desire nothing else
> let us wish for nothing else
> let nothing else please us
> and cause us delight
> except our Creator and
> Redeemer and Savior,
> the one true God.

The center of Saint Francis' life is the Blessed Trinity—our Creator, Redeemer and Savior. And the way into this mystery is not knowledge, but desire, the desire to be united with this God who is three in one. He longed to please and delight this God who delighted and pleased him.

What is my deepest desire? Do I believe with Francis and with Saint Augustine that "Our hearts are made for You, O God, and they cannot rest until they rest in You?"

Today I will _____

_____

A SINGLE-HEARTED LOVE

Saint Francis was intimately united with Jesus—Jesus always in his heart, Jesus on his lips, Jesus in his ears, Jesus in his eyes, Jesus in his hands, Jesus in all the other members of his body. Often when he was on a journey, meditating or singing about Jesus, he would leave the road and start inviting all creatures to praise Jesus.

These words of his first biographer, Brother Thomas of Celano, are the most perfect portrait of Saint Francis. His whole life long he was in love with Jesus, and it gave him the deepest joy, a joy he could not contain. He had to sing aloud his love and invite others to share the sweetness of the Lord. He invited all creatures to praise Jesus, to share his delight in so good and loving a Lord.

How aware am I of Jesus in my daily life? Who is he to me? What portrait could be drawn of my life with Jesus?

Today I will _____

_____

BABY JESUS

Saint Francis used to observe with inexpressible eagerness and above all other solemnities the Birth of the Child Jesus, calling it the feast of feasts on which God, as a little baby, hung upon human breasts. He would avidly kiss pictures of those infant limbs, and his compassion for the child overflowed his heart, making him stammer sweet words, even like a child. The name "Baby Jesus" was for him honeycomb, sweet to the mouth.

Here is the tender Saint Francis, the knight who has turned and become like a little child. So great was his love for the baby Jesus that at the mountain hermitage of Greccio Francis celebrated midnight Mass in a new way, having real animals there, making the Mass a living crib. And it is said that during the Mass a baby appeared on the rock that was serving as the altar; and Francis, who was the deacon of the Mass, took the child in his arms.

What is my attitude toward Christmas? Have I grown sophisticated and cold, too callous to want to take the infant Christ in my arms? Has my Christmas become as commercial as the secular world has made it?

Today I will _____

_____

35

ON CHRISTMAS DAY

If I ever have the opportunity to talk with the emperor, I will beg him, for the love of God and me, to enact a special law: No one is to capture or kill our sisters the larks or do them any harm. Furthermore, all mayors and lords of castles and towns are required each year on Christmas Day to order their subjects to scatter wheat and other grain on the roads outside the walls so that our sisters the larks and other birds might have something to eat on so festive a day. And on Christmas Day, out of reverence for the Son of God, whom, on that night the Virgin Mary placed in a manger between the ox and the ass, anyone having an ox or an ass is to feed it a generous portion of choice fodder. And on Christmas Day the rich are to give the poor the finest food in abundance.

Saint Francis adorns birdbaths all over the world. He is known as the saint of the birds and animals, the lover of nature. And so he was. But he was more. It was because God became one of us in Jesus that all of creation is so precious and good. All creation is made holy in Jesus, and the moment of this great gift is Christmas, the Feast of the Incarnation of God.

When he experienced his great conversion, Francis, who by temperament loved the natural world, began to lift it up to God in gratitude and praise. He did not reject the world as evil; the world was the dwelling place of God.

What is my attitude toward the world God has created and redeemed and sanctified?

This Christmas I will _____

_____

HOLDING BACK NOTHING

O wonderful ascent, O stupendous descent! O sublime humility! O humble sublimity, that the Lord of the universe, God and Son of God, should so humbly hide himself, for our salvation, in what seems to be only a small piece of bread! Look, then, upon the humility of God! And pour out your hearts before him. Humble yourselves that he might exalt you. Hold back nothing of yourselves for yourselves, that he may receive your all who gave his all to you.

This is a signature prayer of Saint Francis. His whole message is contained in this hymn to Jesus Christ, which to comment upon is to cheapen. These words are for praying and contemplating. These words are life for the soul.

What is my signature prayer? What does it say about me?

Today I will _____

_____

A SIMPLE WAY OF LIVING

A Holy Place

This is how the brothers lived in the early days at the Porziuncola, the Little Portion, which is what we called the church of Our Lady of the Angels. Although it was already a holy place, we made it even more holy by constant prayer and silence. If anyone spoke after the time set aside for silence, it was to speak devoutly and discreetly of things pertaining to the praise of God and the salvation of souls.

The little church of Our Lady of the Angels, or the Little Portion, as Saint Francis called it, still draws thousands of pilgrims every year. It is one of three churches that Saint Francis restored with his own hands, and it is next to the place where Saint Francis died.

Saint Francis asked Pope Innocent III for a plenary indulgence, which is an erasing of the temporal punishment resulting from one's sins, for anyone who, repentant of his or her sins, entered this church and prayed for the intentions of the Holy Father. That indulgence remains to this day as thousands cross the threshold of this Little Portion—a testimony to Saint Francis' concern for all people and a witness to the holiness of the first Franciscans who worshiped there in prayer and silence.

Where is my holy place of prayer and silence?

Today I will _____

_____

WORKING WITH OUR HANDS

In order to avoid idleness, we would often go and help
poor farmers work their fields, and sometimes after
work the farmers would share their bread with us for
the love of God. We sanctified ourselves and the place
by these and other virtuous acts.

This charming vignette of how the early Franciscans worked
with their hands and shared the bread of the poor reminds
us of Saint Francis' reverence for work. Work is holy, and we are
sanctified by it if we approach work with the same devotion we
bring to prayer.

How do I view work? What do I need to do to make my work
a prayer?

Today I will _____

_____

THE WAY TO GOD'S KINGDOM

Go, announce peace to all people; preach repentance
for the remission of sins. Be patient in trials, watchful in
prayer, and steadfast in weariness. Be modest in your
speech, responsible in your actions, and grateful to
those who do good to you. And know that in return an
eternal kingdom is being made ready for you.

This exhortation to his brothers is also Francis' exhortation to all
people of good will. These holy words would indeed transform
our world—however large or small that world is—if we but took them
to heart and began, even if just in our own homes, to live them out.

Which words, especially, in this quote from Saint Francis do I
need to put into practice in my own life?

Today I will _____

_____

How to Become a Peacemaker

> The peace you proclaim with words must dwell even
> more abundantly in your heart. Do not provoke others
> to anger or give scandal. Rather, let your gentleness
> draw them to peace, goodness and concord. This is our
> vocation: to heal wounds, to bind what is broken, to
> bring home those who are lost.

Saint Francis defines here the dimension of peacemaking in the brothers' vocation. Peace begins with each brother; and concomitantly, peace begins with each one of us. As the Russian Saint Seraphim once said, "Acquire the spirit of peace, and a thousand souls will be saved around you."

What do I need to do in order to become a peaceful person?

Today I will _____

_____

Embracing Gospel Poverty

God is well pleased with poverty, and above all with voluntary poverty. For my part I possess a royal dignity and special nobility because I follow the Lord, who was rich but became poor for our sakes.

Here Saint Francis gives us his reason for embracing a poor life as his way to God: He was following in the footsteps of the poor Christ.

Who is the Christ I follow? How will I make more earnest my following of the Christ who speaks to me, who inspires me to come after him?

Today I will _____

_____

STRIPPING THE ALTAR OF MARY

> Strip the Blessed Virgin Mary's altar and cart off its furnishings if you cannot otherwise satisfy one who is in need. Believe me, it is dearer to Mary that the gospel of her Son is kept, even if it means stripping her altar, than to see her altar ornamented and her Son neglected.

Saint Francis would strip a beautiful altar dedicated to Mary for the sake of a poor person in order that Christ, whom Francis saw in the poor, be served. It is not ornamentation, but service and love that honor both Mary and her Son. Saint Francis always seems to get to the heart of the matter, as does Jesus when he asks the Pharisees whether it is lawful to heal on the Sabbath. They cannot answer, and Jesus heals anyway, excoriating the Pharisees for their hypocrisy. They will draw an ox out of a ditch on the Sabbath, he says, but hesitate to say whether or not healing is allowed on the Sabbath.

What is my attitude toward the poor? Do I serve them in any way?

Today I will _____

_____

LADY POVERTY

When he lived in this valley of tears, Saint Francis
spurned the poor riches of this world and, longing for
what is higher, panted with all his heart after Lady
Poverty. And when he considered how she had been
the constant companion of the Son of God, he abandoned everything of the world, wanting to bind her to
himself with a chain of eternal love.

Lady Poverty. In his chivalric and poetic way of seeing the world,
Saint Francis sees gospel poverty as a beautiful lady, the bride
of the poor Christ. She is the only one, Dante says, to ascend the
cross with Christ, and now she has been widowed for centuries.
Francis sees her true beauty and chooses to make her his bride and
is proud to wear the livery of Lady Poverty.

Is this Romanticism, or is there something more here? What is
my vision of the poverty of Christ? What image rises to my mind?
Is it a grim image, or a joyful image like that of Saint Francis?

Today I will _____

_____

THE NEED FOR WEAPONS

The Bishop of Assisi once said to Saint Francis, "I think your life is too hard, too primitive. You don't possess anything in this world."

And Saint Francis replied, "My Lord, if we had possessions, we would need weapons to defend them."

In this simple response is wisdom like that of Solomon. How many wars, small and large, could have been avoided if leaders, especially, had been less avaricious of what they presumed belonged to them!

How has my own possessiveness and greed caused small wars in my own family and among my relatives?

Today I will _____

_____

BUSYNESS AND WORRY

We need to be especially alert to the evil subtlety of
Satan. His one desire is to keep us from having a mind
and heart disposed to our Lord and God.

He circles, lusting to snatch away the human heart
by the ruse of some gain or assistance and to stifle
remembrance of the Word and the precepts of the Lord.

He wants to extinguish the light of the human heart,
and so he moves in by means of worldly busyness and worry.

There is the human heart from which, as Jesus says, evil comes.
But there is also a spiritual battle being waged within and
around us that we need to be aware of. Satan, Saint Peter says, goes
about the world like a roaring lion seeking whom he might destroy;
and Saint Francis says that sometimes Satan is more subtle. He uses
some gain or assistance he can offer in order to snatch away our
hearts; or, even more subtly, he plays upon our busyness and worry
to extinguish the light of our hearts. Worry, especially, leaves us open
to desperate reaching out for help from whoever can give it.

Where is my help and who is it that can heal my troubled
heart? "Come to me, all you that are weary and are carrying heavy
burdens, and I will give you rest" (Matthew 11:28).

Is this where I go when I am burdened and heavy-hearted?

Today I will _____

THE MIDDLE WAY

In eating and drinking, in sleeping and satisfying the other necessities of the body, you should take the measure of your own physical tolerance, so that Brother Body doesn't rebel.

You each must know your own physical makeup and allow your body its needs, so that it has strength to serve the spirit. Just as we are bound to avoid overindulgence in food, which harms both body and soul, we must also avoid exaggerated abstinence.

Once when Francis and the brothers were fasting, one of the brothers began to cry out for food late at night, waking the others. Instead of reprimanding the brother, Francis told all the brothers to eat with the brother who had overdone his fasting, thus sparing the brother embarrassment. Then he admonished all of them to know themselves and to take the measure of their own limitations before embarking on a serious fast.

The old saying is, *In medio stat virtus*, or "In the middle way is virtue." Am I moderate in meeting the needs of my body and my soul, or am I extreme?

Today I will _____

_____

SALVATION

Those who are preoccupied only with knowing and pointing out the way of salvation to others, and neglect their own, will arrive naked and empty-handed before Christ's judgment seat.

Salvation begins at home. The great Bishop Helder Camara was once asked what he thought was the greatest obstacle to peace in the world. His answer was immediate: "Yo soy," "I am."

Do I know what is good or bad for others more clearly than I do for myself? Am I judgmental toward others and lenient toward myself? Do I know it all, and do nothing?

Today I will _____

_____

BECOMING A PICTURE OF GOD

In a panel painting representing the Lord or the Blessed
Virgin, it is the Lord or the Holy Virgin who is honored,
while the wood and the painting claim nothing for
themselves. Similarly, a servant of God is a picture of
God in which God is honored for God's favor. And you
may not claim credit that God is pictured through you,
for compared to God, you are less than the wood and
the paint.

This is a beautiful image of how Saint Francis views himself and
exhorts all his brothers to become as they try to represent
Christ to the world. It is to Christ or in this case to his mother that
the honor belongs as well. It is God who is to be pictured in us, not
our own ego standing in the foreground. And because Francis uses
an image, this writing is full of rich overtones and possibilities.

What else do I see in the image Saint Francis uses? What does
the image move me to do?

Today I will _____

_____

DEVOTION

You have as much learning as you put into practice, and
you are as good a witness as you do what you say.

This is a definition of devotion, as it was understood in the Middle Ages. Devotion, according to Saint Thomas Aquinas, is alacrity to do the will of God. You hear the Word of God and immediately attempt to put it into practice.

Do I immediately try to do what I hear God asking of me, or do I procrastinate and find excuses and end up forgetting what it was I was to do?

Today I will _____

_____

SEEING INTO THE MYSTERY

> I, when I was in sin, thought it bitter to look at lepers, and then the Lord led me among them, and I worked mercy with them. And when I left their company, I realized that what had seemed bitter to me had been turned into sweetness of soul and body.

This passage from the Last Testament of Saint Francis is the key to his spirituality: In embracing, for the love of Christ, what seems repulsive, I find instead a physical and spiritual sweetness. Here is the asceticism of Saint Francis that enables one to see beneath the appearance of things into the mystery of God's love within even the most seemingly repulsive of realities.

What is my reaction to the very poor, to those unlike me, to those whose brokenness makes them seem repulsive?

Today I will _____

_____

THE ONE WHO REALLY MATTERS

Blessed are you, servant of God, if you do not consider yourself any better when you are honored and extolled by others than when you are considered low and simple and despised; for what you are before God, that is what you are, and no more.

That no one can enhance or take away who we are before God is an undisputed fact for the believer, but to internalize that truth to the extent that the blame or praise of other human beings is unimportant compared to God's blame or praise is a difficult truth to live. We are influenced by others, we do measure ourselves against those we admire or do not admire; but if what others think inflates or deflates us to the extent that who we are depends on what they think of us, we are losing our true center, who is God, the one who loves us just as we are.

Am I unduly influenced by the opinions of others?

Today I will _____

_____

TRUE AND FALSE RELIGION

Woe to those who are satisfied with the mere appearance of a religious life. They will grow sluggish in their sloth and will not remain steadfast amid the temptations permitted to prove the just; for only those who have overcome the test, after an interval of torment from the malice of the wicked, will receive the crown of life.

How easy it is to pose as a religious person, but at the slightest difficulty or temptation or trial lose our faith in God's providence and love. Virtue requires cooperation with God's grace and a vigilance of heart against becoming so comfortable that one is living an illusion. As someone once said, "The gospel comforts the disturbed and disturbs the comfortable."

Can I try to live one hard saying of Jesus every day?

Today I will _____

_____

MOTHERS, SPOUSES, BROTHERS AND SISTERS OF CHRIST

> We are mothers of our Lord Jesus Christ when we carry him in our hearts and in our bodies, lovingly, and with a pure and sincere conscience, and give birth to him through the working of his grace in us which should shine forth in holy actions that are an example to others. We are spouses of Jesus Christ when our faithful souls are wed to him by the Holy Spirit. We are his brothers and sisters when we do the will of his Father who is in heaven.

This famous Trinitarian passage from Saint Francis is a blueprint for daily living. It speaks for itself. It needs only to be lived out: (1) a pure and sincere conscience, (2) holy actions, (3) espousal to Christ by the Holy Spirit, and (4) doing the will of the Father.

What do I need to do in my own life to become a mother, spouse and brother or sister to Jesus?

Today I will _____

_____

MAINTAINING JOY OF SPIRIT

> The devil is most happy when he can snatch from a servant of God true joy of spirit. He carries dust with him to throw into the smallest chinks of conscience and thus soil one's mental candor and purity of life. But if joy of spirit fills the heart, the serpent shoots his deadly venom in vain.

Joy is the sign of the presence of God because joy is the byproduct of living the gospel and walking in the footsteps of Christ. How disillusioning is the pursuit of happiness for its own sake, for happiness itself is ephemeral. The pursuit of God, on the other hand, brings joy which, unlike happiness, is a state of soul in union with God, not an ephemeral possession like happiness which is sometimes pursued the way one pursues money or fame or success.

What do I need to do to find and preserve joy of spirit?

Today I will _____

_____

PRAYER AND PURITY OF HEART

If you apply yourself to preserving in heart and demeanor the joy that comes from a pure heart and devotion in prayer, the devils can do you no harm. They say: "You are as happy when things are going ill as when all is well, and so we cannot find an opening to enter you and hurt you."

"Blessed are the pure in heart," Jesus says, "for they will see God" (Matthew 5:8). And those who "see" God in prayer have joy whether or not everything is going well in their lives.

Purity of heart and prayer: the two priorities in Saint Francis' life. They sustained him through the greatest physical and spiritual pain and trial.

What are my priorities? Do they sustain me in good times and bad?

Today I will _____

_____

THE GIFT OF WISDOM

Where there is love and wisdom, there is neither fear nor ignorance.

Saint Francis contrasts love and fear, wisdom and ignorance. Love casts out fear, and wisdom prevents ignorance. It is interesting that Francis doesn't say knowledge casts out ignorance, but wisdom. Knowledge is a human acquisition and can lead one away from God, whereas wisdom is a gift of the Holy Spirit and leads us ever closer to God, the source of real knowledge, the knowledge that is wisdom which transforms our life.

Do I pray to the Holy Spirit for the gift of wisdom?

Today I will _____

_____

THE GOOD EXAMPLE OF JOY

If at times temptation and despondency come along to
try me, and I see joy in my companions, then I immediately recover and let go of the temptation or depression. The joy I admire in others restores my own inward
and outward joy.

Saint Francis says so succinctly here how transforming joy is. It
affects not only the joyful person, but those who observe joy
and to know where it comes from. Joy is the reason so many joined
Saint Francis. They saw his joy in poverty, his joy even in living
among and working with the lepers for the love of Christ; and they
wanted that kind of joy.

Have I ever known real joy? If not, where might I find it?

Today I will _____

_____

JOYFUL, JOYFUL WE ADORE THEE

> Since spiritual joy springs from the heart's innocence
> and the purity of incessant prayer, these are the two
> virtues we need to acquire and keep. Then the inward
> and outward joy that I long to see and feel in myself
> and in others will be an edification to neighbor and a
> reproach to the enemy; for sadness is his and his fol-
> lowers' and ours is rejoicing and always being happy
> in the Lord.

Joy again. No wonder Saint Francis is seen as the juggler of God, the one whose very presence and gestures bring joy to others. His is the joy of innocent and total love of God before whom he dances like King David before the Ark of the Covenant.

What joy do I take in God? Do I show this joy in my manner and actions before others?

Today I will _____

_____

TO BE LIKE THE OBEDIENT CHRIST

> As soon as my soul has left my body, strip me naked, as
> I stripped myself before the world, and place me on the
> bare ground. Then leave me there for as long as it takes
> to walk a mile.

Saint Francis wanted to die naked and without anything he could call his own. He wanted to die like Christ on the cross. Always it was Christ, always it was doing what Christ did or what Christ would do. And like Christ, he often had to relinquish his own will in obedience, as Christ was obedient even to death on a cross.

Even on the occasion of this, his last request, he was obedient not to what he wanted but to Brother Elias, who was then the minister of the whole Franciscan community. Brother Elias insisted under obedience that Francis be loaned a habit so that he could be clothed in something that did not belong to him instead of being naked. And Francis rejoiced because even at the end obedience was more perfect than doing one's own will, and obedience preserved his poverty, for the habit was not his own but only loaned to him by his brothers.

How does the obedience of Christ affect my life?

Today I will _____

_____

OUR PERSONAL RESPONSE TO CHRIST

> When he was dying, Saint Francis made clear to his
> brothers the uniqueness of every person's response to
> Christ. He covered the wound in his side with his right
> hand, as if to preserve the seal of his own unique
> response, and he said, "I have done what was mine to
> do; may Christ teach you what is yours to do."

Ernest Hemingway writes in *A Farewell to Arms*, "The world
breaks everyone and afterward many are strong at the broken
places." Saint Francis was one who was wounded for Christ, and
indeed he was strong in the place of his wounding.

What would I cover that is the place of my secret wounding?
How has Christ shown me what to do when I thought I was mortally wounded?

What gesture can I make to the Lord for all he has done for me?

Today I will _____

_____

THE WIDOW'S MITE

Christ's poor one, Francis, possessed nothing but two small coins which he could dispose of with largesse and charity: his body and his soul. But those two mites he offered to God continually for love of Christ; he seemed always to be immolating his body with the rigor of fasting and his soul with the flame of desire: his body, a holocaust outside the court of the temple; his soul, incense offered in the inner temple.

This beautiful passage from Saint Bonaventure's, *Major Life of Saint Francis,* uses the imagery of the poor widow of the Gospel and applies it to Saint Francis, who having nothing of his own, still had two coins to offer God. And like the widow's mite, they were pleasing to God because they were all he had: his body and his soul.

What do I have to offer God that I am willing to give without counting the cost?

Today I will _____

_____

GOD'S WILL

Once when Saint Francis was very ill, one of the brothers asked him what he would prefer to bear, this lingering illness or the suffering of an excruciating martyrdom at the hands of an executioner. Saint Francis replied, "My son, what has always been and still is most dear to me and sweeter and more acceptable is whatever the Lord my God is most pleased to let happen in me and to me, for my only desire is to be found always conformed and obedient to God's will in everything."

In Canto III, line 85 of "Paradiso," Dante writes, "*E'n la sua volontade è nostra pace*," "In his will is our peace." Dante came to know this only after his journey through hell and purgatory into the eternal paradise of heaven. Saint Francis came to know this, as well, through his own journey of conversion and transformation in Christ.

What brings me peace? Do I live the words of the Our Father: "Thy will be done on earth as it is in heaven"? Can I pray with Mary, "Be it done to me according to your word"?

Today I will _____

_____

SAINT FRANCIS AND THE ANGELS

Saint Francis venerated with great affection the angels who are with us on the field of battle and who walk with us in the midst of the shadow of death. We should venerate these companions, he would say, who are with us everywhere, and we should call upon them as our guardians. He used to teach that we should not offend their presence by doing in their sight what we would not do before people.

Saint Francis' devotion to the angels is evident from the beginning of his conversion. He restored with his own hands the little chapel of Our Lady of the Angels; it was an angel on the mountain at Poggio Bustone who assured him that the sins of his past life were forgiven; it was a six-winged seraph with the body of a crucified man who appeared to Saint Francis on Mt. La Verna after which Saint Francis felt and saw in his body the wounds of Christ.

What is my attitude toward angels? Do I believe that they exist and that they protect and guide us on our way?

Today I will _____

_____

How the Devil Works

When you are too sure of yourself, you are less on guard against the enemy. Be alert, therefore, for the devil who, if he can claim even one hair of your head, will lose no time in making a braid of it.

Little things matter, as Saint Francis teaches, with a touch of humor in this passage, especially when it comes to the wiles of Satan. We can be easily compromised by seemingly small decisions or nondecisions that add up until we realize we've changed and are no longer single-minded and pure of heart. We realize that evil has braided together strands as thin as hair and made a braid of the small concessions we have made to evil.

How do I keep my heart and will focused on good?

Today I will _____

_____

AVOIDING ANGER
OVER THE SINS OF OTHERS

No matter how someone else sins, if you let yourself be upset or angered over it, except for charity's sake, you store up for yourself—like a treasure—the sin of the other. But if you do not become angry or indignant over someone else, you are living justly and poorly without claiming anything for your own.

Saint Francis does not tell us to ignore or not see the sins of others. He tells us to avoid becoming angry or upset about what others do, except out of charity, as when our anger derives from and wants only good for the other. It is self-righteous anger that we need to avoid, anger that stores up sin in us not unlike the sin we are upset about.

When I see something that is sinful, why am I upset or angry? Is it out of love for the sinner, or is it because I feel let down or betrayed? Should I not first look more closely at my own life before I become concerned about others?

Today I will _____

_____

HOW TO TELL HOW MUCH PATIENCE YOU HAVE

You do not know how much patience and humility you have as long as everything goes according to your own satisfaction. But when the time comes that instead of receiving your due, you get just the opposite, as much patience and humility as you have then is what you really have, and no more.

J esus is surely Saint Francis' model here—Jesus, of whom Isaiah says,

> *He was oppressed and he was afflicted,*
> *yet he did not open his mouth;*
> *like a lamb that is led to the slaughter,*
> *and like a sheep that before its shearers is silent,*
> *so he did not open his mouth. (Isaiah 53:7)*

How great was the patience and humility of Christ in his passion! How do I react to suffering and reversals in my life?

Today I will _____

_____

TRUE PEACEMAKERS

You are truly peacemakers who, in all you suffer in this
world for the love of our Lord Jesus Christ, preserve
your peace of soul and body.

A repeated theme of Saint Francis: The true peacemaker is one
who is a peaceful person in all the vicissitudes of life.

How peaceful am I? How can I do better? What is the source of
my peace? Is it the gift Jesus gives us after the Resurrection, or is it
some kind of self-discipline or rigorous control of my emotions?

Does it make a difference what gives me peace? How?

Today I will _____

_____

ON BEING SLOW TO SPEAK

> Blessed are you who do not talk in order to gain something and who do not reveal everything about yourself and are not quick to speak, but consider wisely what you are going to say and how you are going to answer.

Here Saint Francis warns of the dangers of the quick tongue, especially when our speech is intended for self-aggrandizement. As always, Saint Francis reverences words and realizes the power of words for good or evil.

Saint James says in his letter, "Anyone who makes no mistakes in speaking is perfect, able to keep the whole body in check with a bridle" (James 3:2).

Do I try to curb my tongue from speaking evil? How have my hasty words led me or others into sin?

Today I will _____

_____

ALL THINGS ARE GOOD

Nothing should be repulsive to the servant of God but sin.

All things are good because God created them, and only sin makes them ugly. The great Franciscan, Saint Bonaventure, defined justice thus: Justice makes beautiful that which has been deformed.

How can my justice restore beauty to things and people I find repulsive? What did Saint Francis do?

Today I will _____

_____

ANTIDOTES TO SIN AND EVIL

Holy Wisdom routs Satan
and his whole malicious band.
Pure Holy Simplicity confounds
all the wisdom of this world
and the wisdom of the flesh.
Holy Poverty confounds cupidity
and avarice and the cares of the world.
Holy Humility confounds pride
and worldly people
and all that is in the world.
Holy Charity routs diabolic
and carnal temptations
and all human fears.

In this wisdom-passage, Saint Francis offers the antidotes to those evils which lead us away from God and which torment our world. These virtues may seem small when we read them on the page, but they can transform our lives.

How do I begin to embrace these virtues in my life? Which virtue applies particularly to me?

Today I will _____

_____

A SIMPLE WAY TO LOVE ONE'S NEIGHBOR

WHO ARE THE MERCIFUL?

Let there be no one who has sinned, no matter how
seriously, who would look into your eyes seeking forgiveness and go away without it. And should the sinner
not seek forgiveness, you should ask him or her if they
want it. And if after that they were to sin a thousand
times, even before your eyes, love them more than me,
for that is how you will draw them to God; and always
have mercy on such as these.

This saying is from Saint Francis' "Letter to a Minister" (a minister being a friar in charge of a community). Though it is intended for the brothers themselves, its sentiment applies to all of us who
need to forgive our brother or sister in order to follow the gospel
teachings of Christ.

In the Our Father Jesus teaches us to pray, "Forgive us our trespasses as we forgive those who trespass against us." The way God
forgives us is the way we are to forgive others, and the way we forgive others is the way we ask God to forgive us.

How merciful am I? Do I strive to forgive those who have hurt me?

Today I will _____

_____

MAKING OUR NEEDS
KNOWN TO ONE ANOTHER

> Be confident in making your needs known to one
> another. For each of you, to the extent that God gives
> you the grace, should love and nourish one another as
> a mother loves and nourishes her child.

This writing of Saint Francis to his brothers is a model of how a Christian community should relate member to member. We are, in Saint Paul's words, "the body of Christ," a reality and a privilege that should make what Saint Francis says here natural and expected of those who love their brothers and sisters in Christ.

Do I hesitate to make my needs known to my brothers and sisters in Christ? How forthcoming am I when others present their needs to me?

Today I will _____

_____

Sharing

I have never been a thief of alms, seeking or using more
than I needed. I always accept less than is necessary, lest
other poor people be cheated of their share.

In a world of graft and greed and corruption, the words of Saint
Francis seem idealistic indeed (or even naïve). But that only says
how far we've fallen from moral principles and justice, not to speak
of true charity that moved so many good people in Nazi concentra-
tion camps, for example, to share their food with others worse off
than they, even though they themselves were starving.

Saint Francis says further that what we share isn't ours anyway;
it is given to us as alms from God, who expects us to share with others what has been so freely given to us.

Do I hoard God's gifts to me? How generous am I with what
God has freely given me?

Today I will _____

_____

WHY WE GIVE

One day Saint Francis heard one of his brothers say to a
poor little man who was begging alms, "How do I know
you're not really rich and pretending to be in need?"

When Francis, the Father of the Poor, heard this,
he was deeply saddened. He severely rebuked the
brother who had dared to utter such words and
ordered him to strip before the beggar and beg his par-
don, kissing his feet.

Who knows whether someone we give alms to is worthy? And
who is ever worthy, including us of the alms God has given
us? We give because Jesus reached out to the poor, because Jesus
became poor for our sake, thus making of every beggar an image of
himself that we can either reach out to for love of Jesus, or not. In
the parable of the Good Samaritan it is the Samaritan who reaches
out to the Jew fallen by the wayside; he reaches out to his so-called
"enemy," one considered unworthy of his attention, one who was to
be spurned.

What is my response to beggars, and even to those posing as
beggars?

Today I will _____

_____

THE POVERTY OF SAINT FRANCIS

Never am I so ashamed than when I find someone more miserably poor than I, for I have chosen Holy Lady Poverty as my delight, and my spiritual and material treasure.

Saint Francis stands as an icon of radical gospel poverty. He is called, *"Il Poverello,"* "the little poor one." And he tried always to be who he professed himself to be. He stands today as the ideal his Franciscan brothers measure their own lives against, asking themselves how far they really measure up to their founder in their own embrace of Lady Poverty. He stands, as well, as an image of Jesus Christ in the Middle Ages, someone universally recognized as an *"Alter Christus,"* another Christ, or as he was also called, *"Speculum Christi,"* Mirror of Christ.

How do I identify with the self-emptying Poor Christ in my own life? Does my lifestyle mirror that of the Christ I strive to emulate?

Today I will _____

_____

WHO ARE OUR FRIENDS?

Jesus Christ, our Lord, whose footsteps we're to follow, called his betrayer "friend" and willingly handed himself over to his crucifiers. Our friends, then, are all those who unjustly inflict upon us tests and ordeals, shame and injury, sorrows and torments, martyrdom and death. They are the ones we should love most, for they are inflicting upon us eternal life.

This is a hard saying. But we instinctively know it is true, difficult and even as impossible as it seems. The way we react to those who persecute and slander us says volumes about who we really are and what we say we believe. Francis is only spelling out for us what Jesus himself said on the Sermon on the Mount: "Blessed are you when people revile you and persecute you and utter all kinds of evil against you falsely on my account. Rejoice and be glad, for your reward is great in heaven" (Matthew 5:11–12).

How do I react to those who contradict, shame or falsely slander me?

Today I will _____

_____

THOSE WHO MIRROR
CHRIST AND HIS MOTHER

When you see a poor person, you are looking at a mirror of the Lord and his poor mother. And in the sick you are contemplating the kind of infirmity he took upon himself for us.

Saint Francis looked everywhere for the imprint of Jesus, and he saw that imprint especially in the poor. Mary, too, was the poor Mary, she who surrendered her life to the good and gracious God whose Spirit descended upon her, impregnating her with the Son of God, whom she in turn surrendered to the Father, handing him over in the temple when he was but a child. Poverty is giving back to God whatever portion we can of the abundance God has given us. Jesus and Mary gave their all.

What can I give?

Today I will _____

_____

How to Live Among Nonbelievers

> You can live spiritually among nonbelievers in two ways. One way is not to enter into arguments or disputes but for the sake of the Lord to be subject to every creature and to acknowledge you are Christians. Another way is to proclaim God's Word when you see it is pleasing to the Lord.

Sometimes the biggest turn-off to nonbelievers is to invade their private space and obnoxiously preach Jesus Christ to them. A better way for some, and usually for most, is to simply witness to our faith by good example: not entering into disputes and arguments, but simply acknowledging that we are Christians. Another way, of course, is to proclaim God's Word, but here, too, Saint Francis adds, "when you see it is pleasing to the Lord."

What good advice is here. Most probably these words were written after Saint Francis returned from the Fifth Crusade, where he had been in dialogue with Sultan Malek-al-Kamil to help bring peace between Muslims and Christians. He even ends this writing with words reminiscent of the Muslim "If Allah wills it."

Is my Christian faith a weapon I use to clobber others? Do I live in a way that inspires others toward reconciliation while at the same time maintaining the truth of who I am as a Christian?

Today I will _____

_____

ADVICE FOR TRAVELERS

I advise, admonish and exhort you in the Lord Jesus
Christ that when you travel through the world you do
not quarrel or argue or judge others; rather, be meek,
peaceful and modest, courteous and humble, speaking
honorably to everyone.

Again Saint Francis encourages us to preach by our example in
word and deed, and he shows us what that example is and
how we are to speak to be disciples of Jesus. How effective is the
witness of a Christ-like life, how ineffective are words when our
actions belie the very message we are proclaiming?

What is more important to me, words or actions? How do the
two become one?

Today I will _____

_____

THE RULE OF PILGRIMS

The rule of pilgrims is this: to take shelter under someone else's roof, to thirst after your homeland and to
make your way in peace.

S aint Francis went about the world as the true pilgrim whom he
describes here. And he encouraged his followers to do the same.
His homeland, of course, is heaven, and the way there is to preserve
our own peace of soul along the way.

What is my homeland? How can I make both this world and
heaven my homeland, one enhancing the other?

Today I will _____

_____

A Peacemaker's Greeting

The Lord revealed to me this greeting, that we should
say, "The Lord give you peace."

How often Saint Francis reiterates the need for peace: peace of soul, peace among people, peace in our relationship to nature, peace in our search for God. For Saint Francis peace is one of the greatest gifts, for in peace all the other virtues grow and because it is the gift Jesus left us after his Resurrection when he says to his disciples, "Peace be with you" (John 20:21). It is this peace of Christ that we in turn are to share with others through the greeting the Lord revealed to Saint Francis, "The Lord give you peace."

Do I wish others peace? How do I show that I am a person of peace?

Today I will _____

_____

THE LOVE OF GOD

> I will never refuse a poor person who begs anything "for the love of God" for how greatly should we love the love with which God loves us.

Once when Saint Francis was a young man selling cloth in his father's shop, a beggar came in and asked for alms for the love of God. The young Francis rudely dismissed the beggar, but then, smitten by remorse, he ran out of the shop and showered the beggar with coins, vowing never to refuse anyone anything who asked "for the love of God." In this writing Saint Francis tells us why.

What does the love of God mean to me?

Today I will _____

_____

How to Love Your Enemy

> You do in fact love your enemy when you do not brood
> over the evil another has done to you, but grieve instead
> over the sin on the other's soul while continuing to act
> with love for the love of God.

How wise these words are, for harboring hurts and brooding over them poisons the soul. We can acknowledge the other's sin but then move on, continuing to live in love, even for the person who has harmed us. Holding on to hurts only hardens the heart and drains us of energy and the joy of living. In hating others in return for their hatred, we give them power over us and end up becoming what we hate in them.

Better to let go and love, after acknowledging the wrong and the sin that caused it, than to brood and become miserable, deprived of the energy that could be used in continuing to love others.

Do I hold on to hurts and refuse to forget or to forgive?

Today I will _____

_____

Praying for the Grace to Forgive

> What we do not fully forgive, do you, O Lord, make us
> fully forgive, so that for your sake we may truly love our
> enemies and devoutly intercede for them with you,
> thereby rendering no evil for evil, but striving in you to
> do good to all.

Saint Francis realizes how glibly or unconsciously we sometimes recite the words of the Our Father, "Forgive us our trespasses as we forgive those who trespass against us." And because he knows how impossible it is to forgive at times, he expands his praying of the Our Father to include this cry for help in forgiving. Saint Francis' words strike home to anyone who has tried to forgive something or someone that seems impossible to forgive.

Do I ask God to help me to forgive when I cannot forgive or find it hard to forgive?

Today I will _____

_____

TRUE LOVE OF NEIGHBOR

Blessed are you who would love brother or sister just as much when they are sick and cannot do anything in return, as when they are well and can.

Here is a definition of love for all ages and seasons. Here is a litmus test for charity. Blessed indeed are they who can live these words of one of Saint Francis' beatitudes.

How faithful am I when someone is no longer able to return my love for them?

Today I will _____

_____

An Antidote to Jealousy

> Blessed are you who are no more puffed up by the
> good which the Lord says and does through you than
> you are by what the Lord says and does through others.

Here is the truly generous heart. Here there is no jealousy, no envy, only rejoicing in all the good God does through me and through others. Here is true humility.

How willing am I to rejoice with others in the good that God does through them, or in the good gifts God bestows on them?

Today I will _____

_____

Doing Good to Others

*Let us love others as ourselves; and if we do not want
to or cannot love them as ourselves, let us at least not
do them evil, but good.*

Here is Francis the realist. OK, if we honestly can't love others
as ourselves, we aren't lost. We can at least not do evil to them,
and we can do good to them. Of course, in doing good to others we
are loving them—maybe not as much as we love ourselves, but we
are loving. How practical this is, how doable!

Is this doable for me? Or am I still unable to be as good to others as I am to myself?

Today I will _____

_____

To Suffer Persecution

If you choose to suffer persecution rather than choose
to be separated from your brothers and sisters, you truly
stand firm in perfect obedience, for you are laying
down your life for them.

These are words that at first sight seem heroic. And yet, though
Saint Francis is speaking to his own brothers, they are words
we all understand and can do if we truly love those we call our
brothers and sisters. Yes, there is heroism here and a kind of martyrdom, but what Saint Francis counsels is not impossible. It is
within our reach if we but love enough.

What am I willing to do for those I love?

Today I will _____

_____

THE SINCERE HEART

Blessed are you who would love and respect brother or
sister as much when they are far away as when they are
present, and would not say anything behind their backs
that couldn't be said with charity face-to-face.

Oh, how profoundly relationships and the world itself would
change if these words were taken seriously.

Can I say that I try to live these words of Saint Francis in my
own life?

Today I will _____

_____

A SIMPLE WAY
OF PRAYER

A Safe Haven

Francis' safe haven was prayer, not prayer for a few minutes, or empty, presumptuous prayer, but prolonged prayer, full of devotion and the serenity of humility. If he began late, it would be dawn before he finished. Whether walking, sitting, eating or drinking, he was rapt in prayer. At night he would retire alone to pray in abandoned, neglected churches. That was how, by God's grace, he overcame many fears and anxieties.

What strikes anyone who reads the life and writings of Saint Francis is how much time he spent in prayer. And as we all know, the measure of our love of anything is how much time we're willing to spend on it and with it. The same is true of our interests and passions. We know what our interest or our passion is by how much time we spend on it.

When I look at my life, what do I spend most of my time on? Is it worth my time? What does what I spend my time on say about me?

Today I will _____

_____

Saint Francis' Prayer Before the Crucifix

This is how Francis prayed before the San Damiano
Crucifix at the beginning of his conversion:
Most High, Glorious God,
enlighten the darkness of my heart,
and give me sound faith,
sure hope and perfect charity,
with understanding and knowledge, Lord,
that I may fulfill your holy and true command. Amen.

How simple, direct and pointed is this prayer. Francis knows
what his spiritual needs are and their order of importance.
When I pray before a crucifix, what do I pray for?

Today I will _____

_____

THE SPIRIT OF GOD

> Pursue what you should desire above all else, namely, to have the Spirit of God and God's grace working in you, to pray always with purity of heart and to have humility, patience in persecution and in infirmity, and to love those who persecute and rebuke and slander you.

In this admonition Saint Francis enunciates the five pillars of his spirituality: The desire for (1) the Spirit of God and God's grace, (2) a pure heart that prays always, (3) humility, (4) patience in persecution and infirmity, and (5) the grace to love those who persecute and rebuke and slander us.

What are the pillars of my own spirituality? What is my deepest desire?

Today I will _____

_____

THE FRAGRANT WORDS
OF JESUS CHRIST

> Receive with divine love the fragrant words of our Lord
> Jesus Christ. And those of you who do not know how
> to read should have them read to you often, and com-
> mit them to memory, and live them unto holiness to the
> end, for they are spirit and life.

In the beautiful phrase, "the fragrant words of our Lord Jesus
Christ," Saint Francis reveals how holistic is his hearing and
internalizing of God's words. They draw him by their fragrance;
they are so sweet to him that he can smell them, taste them. They
can only be received with divine love, which itself is a gift of God.
How delicate this writing is, how reverent it is toward the words
that come to us from the Word, Jesus Christ.

What is my response to God's words? Do they have any sweetness for me?

Today I will _____

_____

Restoring Joy to the Soul

If you are upset for any reason whatever, you should immediately rise up to prayer, and you should remain in the presence of the Most High Father for as long as it takes for God to restore to you the joy of your salvation.

Once we have lost our peace of soul, only God can restore it. Therefore, Saint Francis says, if you feel yourself getting upset for any reason, go immediately to God and remain in God's presence until God restores your joy. Joy, it seems, is the sign that one's peace has been restored; and not just any joy, but the joy that comes from realizing that we have been saved, no matter what it is that is trying to destroy the joy of our salvation.

We know, of course, that clinical depression is an illness and requires professional help, but there are times that we get upset or are downcast for all kinds of human reasons, like envy or disappointment, a sense of failure or loss of faith.

If I have problems or melancholy in my life, do I seek the both human and divine aid in my affliction?

Today I will _____

_____

A SIMPLE PRAYER OF ADORATION

> We adore you, Lord Jesus Christ, here and in all your
> churches in the whole world, and we bless you because
> by your holy cross you have redeemed the world.

This is a prayer that all Franciscans pray wherever they are, and especially when they enter a church or other sacred space. It focuses our prayer on Jesus and reminds us that Jesus is everywhere, that upon entering any space, we need to remind ourselves that it has already been made holy by Jesus Christ's presence there.

What is my response to sacred space? Do I recognize the presence of God in any place I visit or dwell in?

Today I will _____

_____

HUMILITY IN THE FACE
OF GOD'S SPECIAL GIFTS

When you are visited by God in prayer, you should say, "Lord, you have sent me this comfort from heaven, even though I am a sinner and unworthy, and I entrust it to your keeping because I feel like a thief of your treasures." And when you leave your prayer, you should seem to be only a poor little sinner, and not someone especially graced by God.

S aint Francis always tried to keep as holy secrets the special graces he received from God, including the sacred stigmata. He here admonishes his brothers to do the same in order to preserve holy humility and to reverence the intimate touches of God, who is their divine lover.

Do I remember to give thanks for the special touches of God in my life? How do I hold sacred the special experiences I have had of God's presence to me?

Today I will _____

_____

How Saint Francis Prayed Outdoors

When Saint Francis prayed in the wilds and in solitary places, he would fill the woods with sighs, water the earth with tears, beat his breast with his hand, and there, making the most of a more intimate, secret place he often spoke aloud to God. He would give an account to his Judge, entreat his Father, speak with his Friend, and chat amiably with his Bridegroom. Indeed, in order to offer to God with every fiber of his being a single, multifaceted holocaust, he would ponder the many facets of God who is Supremely One.

For Saint Francis God is Judge and Father, Friend and Bridegroom.

Who is the God I pray to? And how do I pray to God when I am alone? Do I seek out secluded prayer-places in nature?

Today I will _____

_____

Saint Francis, A Living Prayer

Often, without moving his lips, Saint Francis would meditate for a long time and, concentrating, centering his external powers, he would rise in spirit to heaven. Thus, he directed his whole mind and affections to the one thing he was asking of God. He was then not so much a man who prayed, as a man who had become a living prayer.

Saint Francis, a Living Prayer. What an icon of this man who seemed always to be in intimate union and conversations with God! Can I emulate such heights of prayer? Where would I begin?

Today I will _____

_____

ANNOUNCING THE TIME OF PRAYER

> Every evening a herald should proclaim or use some
> other signal to announce to all the people that they are
> to render praise and thanks to the Lord God Almighty.

When Saint Francis was in the sultan's camp in Damietta,
Egypt, during the Fifth Crusade, he was deeply impressed
by the muezzin's daily call to prayer. Five times a day faithful
Muslims prostrate themselves in prayer before Allah. When Francis
returned from the crusade he added this passage to his writings.

How do I remind myself to pray? Do I need a regular time each day?

Today I will _____

_____

A Simple Prayer of Adoration

All-Powerful, Most Holy, Most High, Supreme God, all
good, highest good, wholly good, who alone are good,
let us give you all praise, all glory, all thanks, all honor,
all blessing, and all that is good.

This prayer of Saint Francis gives us a glimpse into how he
prayed. The emphasis on God's goodness is striking, as is our
response which gives back to God all that is good.

What is the adjective that defines God for me as personally as
"good" does for Saint Francis? Is there one facet or aspect of God
that most moves me to gratitude and praise?

Today I will _____

_____

A PERFECT PRAYER

All-powerful, eternal, just and merciful God, grant that we poor creatures might do by your grace what we know you want us to do, and to want always what is pleasing to you, so that interiorly cleansed and enlightened and inflamed by the fire of the Holy Spirit, we might follow in the footsteps of your Beloved Son, our Lord Jesus Christ, and by your grace alone come to you, O Most High, you who live and reign glorified in perfect Trinity and in simple Unity, God Almighty forever and ever. Amen.

What further word could be added to this almost perfect prayer, except to pray it devoutly?
Is this a prayer I could pray every day?

Today I will _____

_____

THE IMPORTANCE OF SILENCE

Where there is quiet and meditation, there is neither
preoccupation, nor dissipation.

Saint Francis was so insistent on the need for quiet and meditation
that in his *Rule for Hermitages,* he sent his brothers off two by two
to pray in places of solitude. One was to act as son and enter into solitude and silence, and the other was to act as mother, guarding the son's
solitude and bringing him food and other necessities at appointed
times. Then, after a while, the brothers would exchange places, the son
becoming the mother, and the mother becoming the son.

How much value do I place on solitude and silence and who
will protect it for me?

Today I will _____

_____

BECOMING GOD'S SERVANT

> I prayed that God would deign to show me when it is I
> am God's servant and when not, for I want nothing else
> but to be God's servant. And the Lord answered most
> graciously: "Know that you are truly my servant when
> you think, do and say what is holy."

Here is Francis, the practical saint. There is no secret here about what it takes to be God's servant.

What does it mean to think, do, and say what is holy? It is, as Saint Paul says, all about love, but a very special kind of love, the divine gift of charity:

> *Love is patient; love is kind; love is not envious or boastful or*
> *arrogant or rude. It does not insist on its own way; it is not irri-*
> *table or resentful; it does not rejoice in wrongdoing, but rejoices*
> *in the truth. It bears all things, it believes all things, hopes all*
> *things, endures all things.*
>
> *Love never ends.... And now faith, hope, and love abide,*
> *these three; and the greatest of these is love.* (1 Corinthians
> *13:4–8; 13)*

Is this something I can do?

Today I will _____

_____

CONTEMPLATION

The pure of heart are those who never cease adoring
and looking with pure heart and soul upon the Lord
God living and true.

What a description of contemplation! This looking anyone can do and in so doing, however imperfectly at the beginning, will gradually become pure of heart.

How can we find time in our daily lives to look upon God? And where can we look? Jesus tells us where he is and we can see him: "I was hungry and you gave me food, I was thirsty and you gave me something to drink, I was a stranger and you welcomed me, I was naked and you gave me clothing, I was sick and you took care of me, I was in prison and you visited me" (Matthew 25:35–36).

Can I contemplate God this way?

Today I will _____

_____

THE GRACE OF PRAYER

We should desire the grace of prayer above everything
else, and in every way possible.

For Saint Francis prayer is the indispensable foundation of our
life with God because it was through prayer that he was able to
let God change his heart; it was through prayer that he was able to
meet Christ in the leper; it was through prayer that he learned what
he was to do to restore God's house.

How can I take prayer more seriously in my own life?

Today I will _____

_____

TRUE AND FALSE PIETY

There are those who apply themselves unceasingly to prayer and to the responsibilities of office; they abstain and mortify their bodies often; but for one word that seems injurious to their person or any other thing that might detract from them, they are scandalized and thoroughly upset. These are not poor in spirit.

Saint Francis knew from his own experience the disconnect that sometimes happens to those who seemingly are rapt in God through prayer and devotion to their responsibilities and yet are really rapt in their own image of themselves, their own importance. Any challenge to that false piety brings out the truth and they see how pride has been the real foundation of their piety. They are not the poor in spirit of whom Jesus says, "[T]heirs is the kingdom of heaven" (Matthew 5:3). How subtly pride insinuates itself into our prayer and holy ministry!

How can I heed Saint Francis' warning and become poorer in spirit?

Today I will _____

_____

A SIMPLE WAY TO LOVE GOD'S CREATURES

Saint Francis' Love of Creatures

Saint Francis embraced all things with an unheard of love and devotion, speaking to them of the Lord and exhorting them to praise God. He spared lights, lamps and candles, refusing to be responsible for extinguishing their light which he saw as a symbol of the eternal light.

We are so bombarded with images of violence and insensitivity toward nature that these words about Saint Francis may seem overwrought. But are we perhaps too far to the extreme of indifference and even violence toward nature?

How far has my own insensitivity toward nature removed me from the world God asks me to nurture and protect?

Today I will _____

_____

A LADDER TO GOD

Saint Francis praised the Artist in every one of the Artist's works; whatever he found in things made, he referred to their Maker. He rejoiced in all the works of God's hands, and with joyful vision saw into the reason and cause that gave them life. In beautiful things he came to know Beauty itself. To him all things were good. They cried out to him, "The One who made us is infinitely good." By tracing God's footprints in things Saint Francis was following God wherever God led. Francis made from created things a ladder to God's throne.

What is our ladder to God? Do we, like Saint Francis, see in nature a pathway to God? Or do we even notice nature?

Sometimes, especially when we can't seem to pray, the best thing we can do is simply take time to do nothing but look at flowers or at birds or at the sky.

One can look at three roses in a vase and feel one's heart lifting. Two pink roses and one yellow. That's all one needs to make a ladder to God. The Trinity is there and the yellow rose is Jesus of the golden crown, his shining Resurrection.

What more do I need to pray?

Today I will _____

_____

TILLING AND PRESERVING THE EARTH

Saint Francis called all animals "brother" or "sister" and
we read in his story how even wild animals came run-
ning to him as their friend and companion.

Is nature for us merely a thing? Or are animals and plants living
creatures that we embrace as our brothers and sisters? Why does
it matter what we think of the natural world?

If the natural world only serves our need to dominate instead
of our need to name and cherish, then one of God's first purposes
in creating us is dismissed: "The LORD God took the man and put
him in the garden of Eden to till it and keep it" (Genesis 2:15).

What have I done to insure the tilling and the preserving of
the earth?

Today I will _____

_____

How Creatures Teach Us

Consider, O human, the wondrous dignity God has conferred upon you. God created you and formed your body in the image of God's Beloved Son, and your soul in God's own likeness. Still, all creatures under heaven serve and know and obey their Creator in their own way better than you do.

Saint Francis meditated on God's creatures all his life long. They spoke to him of his Creator, they were obedient in ways he was not, and they reminded him that he, too, was a creature like them who needed to remember why God created him and what he was to do to be obedient to his creaturehood. He used to pray, "Who are you, O God, and who am I, your poor lowly creature?"

What do other creatures teach me about God and about my own created being?

Today I will _____

_____

BROTHER SUN AND BROTHER FIRE

At dawn, when the sun rises, everyone should praise
God who has created Brother Sun for our service, for
through him our eyes light up the day; in the evening,
when night descends, everyone should praise God
through Brother Fire, for through him our eyes light up
the night. We are all, as it were, blind and it is through
these two brothers that the Lord gives light to our eyes.
We should praise the Lord, then, in a special way for
these creatures and for the others, too, who serve us
day by day.

It may seem such a small, insignificant thing to praise God for
creatures; but as the French novelist Georges Bernanos writes,
"Little things seem nothing, but they give peace, like those meadow
flowers which individually seem odorless but all together perfume
the air."

Do I even notice the sun in the morning? Do I give any attention to fire? Do I thank God for anything other than what these two
elements do for me? How self-centered is my world? How can my
response to God's creation free me from my self-absorption?

Today I will _____

_____

THE LESSON OF THE ALMOND TREE

> One day Saint Francis was filled with joy because he was beginning to enjoy God in all creatures. He went through the streets singing and inviting everyone to sing along with him. Then he came upon an almond tree, and he said, "Brother Almond, speak to me of God." And the almond tree blossomed.

What is it that the almond tree said to Francis in simply blossoming?

We all have only to be who God created us to be. To let unfold the natural growing into maturity and fruitfulness is the most important gift we have to give. To learn how to facilitate that growth, how to release the potential of who we can be is wisdom.

Nature is one of the deepest sources of this wisdom if only we begin to observe what is there before us. We have only to contemplate any one thing until it begins to open up and reveal its own unique self, its own unfolding. As the Jesuit poet Gerard Manley Hopkins once said, "If you look hard at anything, it will look hard at you."

How does the lesson of the almond tree blossoming apply to me in my relationship with nature and with myself?

Today I will _____

_____

BROTHER BIRDS

*My Brother Birds, you should always praise and love
your Creator. God covered you with feathers and gave
you wings to fly with and granted you a kingdom of
pure air. God cares for you, too, without any worry on
your part, though you neither sow nor reap.*

Have we grown too sophisticated to talk to birds and animals, to
plants and fish and to the heavens? What is Saint Francis really doing when he talks to the animals? Why can't we do the same?

Why, indeed? People talk to their pets, people talk to plants;
and somehow in the tone of voice or warmth of breath the animal
or plant is affected. More importantly, we are affected when we
come out of ourselves to notice God's creatures and talk or sing for
them; or like Saint Francis, to praise God for them, through them,
and with them.

What can I learn from Saint Francis talking to the birds and
encouraging them to love and praise their Creator?

Today I will _____

_____

SISTER LARK

Sister Lark has a hood like a friar and is a humble bird who gladly goes in search of any little grain, and even if she finds something in the garbage, she picks it out and eats it. In flight she sweetly praises God like a good religious who, detached from worldly things, turns ever toward heaven and who longs only to praise God.

Are we always complaining about our lives? Do we feel cheated if we're not rich or famous, handsome or beautiful, brave or strong? What does the symbol of Saint Francis' Sister Lark tell us about what we, too, need to do?

How many stories there are of the poor person whose heart is grateful for the smallest gift while the rich person complains, is never satisfied, no matter how much is given or earned. We need only think of Charles Dickens' beloved *A Christmas Carol*—of Ebenezer Scrooge, Bob Cratchit and Tiny Tim.

What is my story?

Today I will _____

_____

LITTLE SISTER CICADA

One day when Saint Francis came out of his cell, he saw a cicada on a branch of the fig tree that grew beside the door. The cicada was so close he could have reached out and touched it, but instead he stretched out his hand and said, "Come to me, little Sister Cicada." And immediately it jumped down upon his finger. Saint Francis then began stroking the cicada with a finger of his other hand and inviting it to "Sing, little Sister Cicada." And as soon as the cicada heard his words, she began to sing, consoling Francis and moving him to praise God. He held the cicada in his hand for a good hour and then put it back on the branch of the fig tree where he had found it.

What does this little vignette tell me about contemplation, about waiting and looking and letting the other come to me? What does it say about taking time to "waste time" with a cicada or any of God's creatures?

Today I will _____

_____

THE LAMB OF GOD

One day Saint Francis found a shepherd feeding a herd of goats. Among the goats there was one little lamb, and when Saint Francis saw it, he stopped and, moved inwardly with sorrow of heart, he said to the brother who was with him, "Do you see this sheep that walks so meekly among the goats? I tell you that our Lord Jesus Christ walked in the same way meekly and humbly among the Pharisees and chief priests. Therefore, I ask you, my son, for the love of him to have pity with me on this little sheep. Let us pay the price and lead her away from among these goats."

Saint Francis saw symbols of Christ everywhere. Especially in nature, the images Jesus used in the gospel leapt out at him and he was moved to praise.

What moves me to praise? How often does my prayer consist in praise of the good God who created such wonders for us? Do I see Christ in any of God's creatures?

Today I will _____

_____

BROTHER RABBIT

One of the brothers brought Saint Francis a little rabbit
that had been caught in a trap. When Saint Francis saw
the rabbit, he said, "Brother Rabbit, come to me. Why
did you allow yourself to be tricked like this?" And the
rabbit jumped from the brother's arms and fled to the
saint and lay in his lap as the safest place possible. After
he had lain there for a while, the holy father Francis,
caressing it with motherly affection, released it so it could
return free to the woods. But every time Saint Francis
placed it on the ground, the rabbit turned and jumped
into his lap. Finally Saint Francis commanded one of the
brothers to take it to a nearby wood and release it.

Though Francis loved creatures and even spoke to them, he
never held on to them or tried to keep them from being who
they were. He loved them and praised God through them and with
them, but he did not try to make them his own.

How possessive am I of the gifts that God has given me in other
creatures, human or otherwise? Can I release them and let them live
free of my control of them?

Today I will _____

_____

BROTHER FLOWERS

Saint Francis told the brother gardener not to plant the whole garden with food, but to set aside a plot for those plants which in their season would bloom with Brother Flowers. He said the reason the brother gardener should plant this pretty little flower bed with its sweetly scented herbs and flowering plants was because it would invite all who saw it to praise God; for every creature says, "God made me for you, human!"

Isn't it beauty most of all, beauty without any useful purpose other than itself, that lifts our hearts to God? To deprive ourselves of beauty is to deprive ourselves of an important reminder of God, who is Beauty itself.

How utilitarian am I in my response to nature? Must everything somehow serve my need for food? For clothing? For shelter? For comfort?

Today I will _____

_____

Sister Swallows

Once, when Saint Francis was preaching, he could not be heard because of the chattering of a flock of swallows building their nests there. So Saint Francis said to the birds:

"My Sister Swallows, you have had your say. Now it's my turn. Be quiet now and listen to the word of the Lord."

Then to the astonishment of the people standing about, the little birds fell silent and did not move until Saint Francis had finished preaching.

This is one of the stories of Saint Francis that some find sentimental and childish, and yet how many of us know people who have a way with animals, like "horse whisperers," for example, and those who seem to communicate with their pets in very real ways. Perhaps we all need more of what the Rumi translator Coleman Barks said of Saint Francis: He "was so empty of nervous haste and fear and aggression that the birds of the air would light on him."

Do I even notice the birds? And if I do, would I take the time to lose myself in the birds the way I lose myself in a weekly television series?

Today I will _____

_____

BROTHER FISH

Once when Saint Francis was sitting in a boat on a lake near Rieti, a fisherman who had just caught a large carp rowed over and kindly offered him the fish. Saint Francis accepted it joyfully and gracefully, and immediately began calling it "Brother." Then he placed the fish gently in the water and began praising the name of the Lord. And all the while that Saint Francis prayed, the fish continued to play beside the boat and would not leave until the saint finished his prayer and gave it permission to leave.

This is every fisherman's story, except, of course, that Saint Francis returned the fish to the water. One need not be extreme or weird here and say that no one should go fishing or eat the fish he or she catches; this story tells of Francis' reverence for creation. Perhaps, like Native Americans, we could ask forgiveness of the game we kill before we take its life and assure it that every part will be used and respected for its value. Perhaps we need to be reverent toward every creature we kill in order to eat, or every creature that is served up to us already dead and butchered or pulled from the ground. Reverence. The virtue of the saint.

How reverent am I toward the animal world? Do I take them for granted when they're served up as food for me?

Today I will _____

_____

LARKS ASCENDING

The larks are friends of daylight and shun the shadows of twilight. But on the eve that Saint Francis passed from this world to Christ, just as twilight was descending, the larks rose up to the roof of his cell and began circling it with clamor of wing beat and song.

What a fitting gesture from the larks he loved and even spoke to when he was alive. They symbolize all of creation that Francis had learned to call Brother and Sister.

Who will be there for me when I die? Who have I taught to praise God, even in my death?

Today I will _____

_____

THE CANTICLE OF THE CREATURES

Most High, all-powerful, good Lord,
Yours is praise, glory, honor,
and every blessing.
They belong to you alone, Most High,
whose name no one is worthy to utter.

And praised be you, my Lord,
with all your creatures,
especially Sir Brother Sun,
who makes the day
and enlightens us through you.
He is lovely and radiant and grand;
and he heralds you, his Most High Lord.

Praised be you, my Lord,
through Sister Moon and the stars.
You have hung them in heaven
shining and precious and fair.

Praised be you, my Lord,
through Brother Wind,
through air and cloud,
calm and every weather
that sustains your creatures.

Praised be you, my Lord,
through Sister Water,
so very useful, humble,
precious, and chaste.

Yes, and praised be you, my Lord,
through Brother Fire.
Through him you illumine the night,
and he is handsome and merry,
robust and strong.

Praised be you, my Lord,
through our Sister Mother Earth,
who nourishes us and teaches us,
bringing forth all kinds of fruits
and colored flowers and herbs.

O, and praised be you, my Lord,
through those who for your love
forgive one another
and bear sickness and trials.
Blessed are they who endure in peace;
they will be crowned by you, Most High!

Praised be you, my Lord,
through our Sister Bodily Death,

from whom no one can escape.
How dreadful for those
who die in mortal sin,
how lovely for those
she finds living
your Most Holy Will,
for the second death
can do them no harm.

O praise and bless my Lord,
thank him and serve him
humbly but grandly!

Saint Francis' "Canticle of the Creatures," sometimes called, "The Canticle of Brother Sun," is the first great Italian poem. Sung in medieval Umbrian dialect, it expresses the depths of Saint Francis' vision of the ultimate reconciliation of all creation, using the classical elements of the universe, earth, water, air and fire. He calls them each "brother" and "sister," and he praises God through them. He adds a stanza on forgiveness and a final stanza on Sister Death, thus completing the task of every human being: to love and praise God through God's creation, to forgive one another as God has forgiven us and to embrace death as our dear sister who leads those who have done God's will into the paradise prepared for them from all eternity. It is a poem and a song of the soul's journey into God. Though we no longer have the music that Francis sang to this extraordinary poem, we have the original Umbrian words which, though untranslatable (as any poem is ultimately untranslatable), are rendered here in an English approximation. Pray it, say it, sing it, live it.

Today, and always, I will praise _____

_____